Stwe G

UP IN THE AIR

Steve Griffin is a poet and novelist. Born in Eastbourne in 1967, he has a BA in English from Southampton University and an MSc in Environmental Management from Stirling University. After leaving Scotland he worked for an environmental organisation in Wales, where amongst other things he ran *Poetry and Place* projects in which children's poems were inscribed on public artworks. Afterwards, he spent six months travelling around Burma, Nepal, Thailand and India, which inspired him to write the young adult adventure series, *The Secret of the Tirthas*.

Steve Griffin's poetry has been published in over twenty anthologies, competitions and periodicals including *Poetry Ireland, The New Welsh Review, The Rialto, Magma* and *Poetry Scotland.* He now lives in the Surrey Hills with his wife and two sons.

To hear about new writing, please send an email to stevegriffin40@outlook.com with a request to subscribe to his mailing list. You can also find out more on his website, steve-griffin.com, and connect with him using the social media handle @stevegriffin40 on Instagram, Facebook and Twitter.

Up in the Air

Steve Griffin

by Steve Griffin

FICTION

The Secret of the Tirthas series:
The City of Light
The Book of Life
The Dreamer Falls
The Lady in the Moon Moth Mask
The Unknown Realms

for Anna,
ever my inspiration

Contents

7

v. Air

Acknowledgements

Acknowledgements are due to the editors of the following publications where some of these poems first appeared: *Poetry Ireland, New Welsh Review, The Rialto, Magma, Tandem, Other Poetry, Orbis, Envoi, The Magazine, Staple, Poetry File, Poetry Scotland.*

See things differently

i. Air

The Touch of Birds

At the crest of the hill,
a wall-stitched woodland fringe;
beneath, the white heads of two dozen gulls,
iconic on the broken soil.
Waiting for the tractor,
groaning up the hill.

It comes, with its blunt, hefty blades
turning up the clay, revealing
a juicy crop of worms.

Then the birds lift
across the buzzing forest green –
drift apart, and join –
go with them –

because you can –

go –

Weather Map

I love the blue and green weather map,
    its spindly augur.

She stands beside it, what we know is not
really there – broad Britain, so much rock, trees
                  villages and towns
teeming beneath its battered outline. I am ready
                for the quickening.

Tell me about Britain's weather,
the pressure we are about to bear.
Tell me of squalls on moorlands in the night,
              soaking into huddled sheep.
Tell me of the summer sun

            warming zigzags

on adders' backs.
Tell me
    how hot it is in Manchester.

Her fingers reach up, stroke two hundred miles
                  of Wales.
There will be snow on frosted hills.

Some atmospheric fog
            will go on loan to Scottish lochs.

That night we sleep against a storm in the eaves,
wake in London, on the banks of the Wandle.
You get up, throw back the curtains
                to show me the weather –

full sunlight,
    slipping on the spittle of webs

blinking
    on the morning river.

The Wandle Geese

Bright brown, white, and black
straining, swift
against the uppermost limits
of the river-channel's air
honking
and half-honking

come the throat-stretched geese,
nature regenerate,
unmade,
singing the quality
that flies ahead of itself

roll-calling the bounty
of the nettle-thick banks

stamping their mark
on the ducks and the coots
championing the ever-ready

and demanding renewed assault
on the beauty and mystery
grown over within.

The Cormorants

If I could be whisked away warmly
from this spinning sack of sleep
I would rise through the hollow rain-wet night
past the soft-touching leaves of trees
and travel beyond this cosy land.

With arms stretched out through the cold
I would come to the dark salt sea
chopping remorselessly at the moon,
and finally to Iona of peace,
and the unnamed rocks about it.

And there I would find the cormorants, with
black bills hunched in a cloak of grey, watching
watching what? as they soak
with rain and briny spray, watching for
the tides that make and seek them.

Scarecrow

The crow is not itself
just as I am not myself alone –
some of me is stolen
by that shrewd, wheeling eye.

What do I look like in crow?
Dumb, slow, stumbler on a field
of plenty, just trouble enough
to keep an eye on.

It sits there on my fencepost,
careless that it contravenes the good of me.
Watching me, utterly
unafraid of me.
Watching me, my enemy.

Watching me as I pierce
the slopping, inert earth with my cross
and dress its stick arms with shredded sacks.
And it doesn't caw or blink
as I settle on the upright pole a pumpkin
and on that a black, shapeless hat.

The light on the winter field fails.
The crow's wings stretch out,
pass up through me
as I walk, unsteadily, home.

Leaving my scarecrow in the field.
Alone with the crow.

Bird Garden, Hong Kong

In the new Bird Garden
on Yeung Sen Street
very old men
gaze at caged songbirds.

One lifts a bell-shaped dome
from a branch –
holds it above his chest,
level with his earth-worn face.

There. Its sudden trill
could be the sound of hope
played backwards,
bright beads falling from the string of time –

or the beauty of things forgotten.

Up in the Air

Be the antelope on the plain,
mind without thought,
mild brown eyes
gazing up –

Or the Bodhisattva on a mountain,
in the zone where
past and future
are firmly in place.

Or even Da,
in Eastbourne '75,
on a sun lounger,
fag on chest

the noise of Caen '44 behind,
heat all around,
and nothing yet
to come –

Da thinks not,
says not,
and, like smoke
from his fag,

is up in the air,
the thin, salt-blue air.

In Praise of Steven Bradbury

— Winter Olympics, Salt Lake City, 2002

Oh, just to be Steven Bradbury
to put in all that effort
learn how to turn grip into slip
willing the muscles to work
almost on air –

the subordination of strength and will
to something more ethereal,
more transcendent in us –

this workman of the ice
who always came last
and now, again, in Salt Lake City, clearly
behind his Chinese, US, etcetera competitors –

surely no chance in hell
of winning, only then to see
the whole damn power-pack collapse,
trip up on its own success,
a jumble of stretched yellow lycra,
half-melon helmets
and upturned blades –

24

and you, Steven Bradbury,
swinging your fist in triumph
glancing back in amazement –

and now the fire
splodges your cheeks –

Regeneration, Colliers Wood

Flowing
like the river
going home
and crushed up
like the river

in between
High Path
and the Savacentre
half my eye
snaps a bolt of blue –

did a kingfisher
release the river
just for one moment?

And, if it wasn't the kingfisher
how come the river
is here with me
in my living room

flowing
on the other side of now?

ii. Love

Wedding Song

And as they came out into the gladbright day
the light sprang up in their eyes
for all the crowd to see
that they were sunmade –

and the day danced
danced through the eyes of lovers
danced because there is never
anything except beginning
and never is it known more
than on this day –

and we all would follow
swept up like the spangled leaves
of glorious trees,
savouring their sunshine

and they came out singing
and they came out dancing
and they came out thinking
that they'd never been like this before –

and we would all be
blown gaily through the gorgeous day
as if time were nothing but air –

unless we were now
to stop

for just this one moment
and think each of ourselves
all here now
in our hearts

alive

and real as love.

Diaspora of Light

Stretching up she twists the slats

and, having combed
all that empty space
failed to catch
retreating galaxies
collapsing stars

bounced off
or come to nothing
on nameless, burnt out rocks

at last the barriers down
light
finds perfect resting place
on her naked skin

glories with silent fanfare

and begins its transmission
of the precious stuff, metals
gold, silver, platinum and bronze

from the places
where her stomach twists
her arm curves against the air;

from the coppery shift of her hair,
the coral blue-grey blink
of her perfect eyes.

Small Boy's Poem

I am small and I am precious and I am
growing up in Merthyr Vale which is called
'Ynysowen' which is next to Aberfan.
Mrs Thomas is my headteacher and she is
very nice but she tells me that I have
a loud voice for someone so small because I am
just the smallest boy in my class
although Peter Ryan is
nearly as small as me.

I also like Mrs Jones who's my class teacher
especially when it's nearly end of term
and we all go out on the playing field
for games and we have one sack race and
one egg and spoon race before it
starts to rain and we have to go back in
but it doesn't matter because
the teachers are all being funny
which makes me want to

run around and go 'yaroo'
which I do and that's when Mrs Thomas
calls me over and puts her arm around me
and tells me that
I have a loud voice
for one so small as me
and looks at me like my mum does
when she tells me
that I'm precious.

Cats Love Me

you say as we pass one on a garden wall,
a mottled sack of idleness.
But as you proffer a mittened hand
a row of tiny white fangs
springs out amidst the fluff.

Turning a bend we spot a ginger puss
pulled tight across the path
by a squirrel, nibbling acorns, just yards away –
aware of us, yet ignoring us.

We walk towards him
and he holds his pose
making increasingly fine judgements
as we approach.

Now the cat's dilemma –
to display, indiscreetly, his viciousness,
the bloody side of his nature,
or else to quickly don
the soft known coat of civilisation.

And, at the last moment, he's there
beneath your stroking hand
wrapping the glad scarf of his tail
around your forearm –

lifting up his face to you
as if he were a proud young prince
waiting to be kissed.

The Old Man

In stride pale valleys grow before us,
smoothed between slumbering beasts,
exciting strange pools of thought;
after roaming the Old Man and returning
like water we fall together
by a crumbling river and you sing,
a silly song, into my ear
as I rest my thoughtless head in your lap.

What are you to me?
Dreaming child, self-absorbed,
before eroded thoughtways
you sing the possibility of freedom.

Albatross Statue, Wellington

And then I came across the statue of the albatross,
the bird that flies above cliff and deep water
like everyone dreams to fly
but is ungainly, glue-
footed and beak-weighted
on the earth.

That bird whose beauty
is in the soft white head and self-possessed eye,
the bird that mates just once for life
when each partner
flies out to discover
new currents, new continents,
but always comes back to the other.

The bird that should be flying now
but instead is stone.

Zipping and Hooking

Zipping and hooking your dress is the best.
Anyone might be in the room
when you make this most legitimate request,
turn your back towards me
and feel the shiver of my lust.

So my steadied fingers are allowed
to bind the soft white-pink of your flesh
with each struggling
notch
of the black plastic
zip

which, with a final pinched hook,
comes to rest between two butterfly wings
of perfect bone
below ten thousand threads
of perfumed hair

in the exact most painful place
my lips will never touch.

The Jersey Lily

Being so tired
that her body's tide shook then drowned
all her melancholy naggings,
she found herself approaching
her instant brilliance –

her eyes clothed themselves
in colours incandescent and bright
and a hopeful smile
grew and crinkled
on her radiant face.

Her laugh came like
a sudden snake
which kissed instead of bit
and her gentle touch spread flowers
where it landed.

How could I ever be doubtful
when her surging joys rode the air,

trampling my foolish and thankless pretenders,
and leaving me with
all the startling pleasures
I could be.

Hedgelayer

A man, a man I could have loved
starts to shade, to shade the morning mist.

He is beating stakes, stakes into the clay
forcing them past stones, stones and steady roots,
the things weak within the earth
and the things that hate to move.

As I approach he takes his shape assuredly
from the frail and wet white air,
a seamster weaving hazel whips through the hedge,
outwitting the final challenge of scratch and rip.

In defeat the hawthorn rests its useless claws
uneasily against itself, uncertain how to act.
Then feels the sap rise, rise again in its veins,
and knows that it is elect.

The man who was saved

by a fire-fighter at the Marriott Hotel on 9/11 was
OK before; before he'd never shown anyone any
affection and expected none himself but when an
unknown man, a stranger, did that to him – saved
him, without him asking – he found that something
shut away for a long time, so long it might as well
have been forever, came out and that's what has
made him cry each time he watches the news, what
has made him alive and weak. He loves being weak.

'She being dead yet speaketh'

just before I wake or when the dog
looks suddenly up from cracking its bone.
When my name sung by her voice
seeps through the wood in the house.
When I run to the phone,
thinking that it's her.
Behind the confusion
of a stranger's piped words.

In the blaze of the baby's hair
as she sprawls beneath blue bay windows
I hear her still speaking
telling me always, telling me nothing,
making me feel, before it bursts,
like light.

Please, stop sending the cards.
She is still talking.
I am all right.

Necessity

She wakes up with a sudden start
that may have been a noise
and her body begins to lock itself
with a thousand flowing could-bes.

She's seized by an implacable fear
in the rare vividness of the night
in a mind more bright and quick
than daylight ever sees.

Holding her breath, she counts intently
the fluttered moments of nothing,
squeezes hard on rigid muscles
as the empty house sighs and creaks.

It is a patient waiting for grace.
For something that loves her very deeply
is slowly discovering the combination
to put her back to sleep.

Sausage, Chips and Beans

The four old women
in Fern Hill Community Centre
start to shake
their glass salt cellars.

Salt up, salt down
salt up, salt down
back and forth
across four sausage, chips and beans.

'I like my salt,'
smiles one, 'You do,'
says another, arms
rocking in unison.

I am still watching.
Some dots of white
fly outwards, bounce
and slide on the blue formica.

When they have finished
I ask one
to pass the salt
if she wouldn't mind.

I spin it quickly, once,
over my chips,
watched by four sets
of bemused spectacles.

Muse

You are the start of things
you bring more than I ever wished for
you bring me blue ammonites from the shore
dark berries from the garden
and you show me the way
through fern filled woods
you bring fresh love
you bring fresh time
with you the past is retrieved
and the future is spellbound
you make the present alive
you have a sunband in the soul
and you sparkle with numinous light
you fill my life with love and surprise
and you make me more
than I was before
and, in case you never knew,
you are my muse
I write for you.

iii. Image

On Justice

– portrait of Margareta van Eyck, Groeninge Museum,
Bruges

Here I am
every bit as real
an image as you.
How come you
get to breathe?

Look at this mastery,
the skill applied here, and here,
the dab of light
on the flesh
at the corner of the eye –

How good are you?
What do you do so well?
Why is it oxygen burns
when it touches
the blood in your lungs?

Self Portrait

His face is alive with stitching,
and all the colours under the sun.
Like a wheat field scored by a gusting wind,
or a closing pride of unseen predators.
And from somewhere in the field –
white and green.

The face a ginger cat-monster's face,
a knitting of beauty and beast.
The stitched lips unable to utter
something in the mind made true.
And leaping from the apparition's glare –
grey and blue.

Or the face that of a crash victim,
weak flesh mended by a Frankenstein –
the blood still congealed,
the beard red, from the knife's touch.
And somewhere on the ear, near the top –
a little more red.

From his face he's made his own straw doll,
set it in motion on the canvas
with a thousand frenzied strokes.
So now it's alive, alive with stitches,
a witch's doll, and he's pierced it
with those smooth, colourless eyes.

The Ogwr-Garw Display

The trees present themselves to us
as frozen moments of ecstasy –
in leaping for the sky
a vicious god has had them petrified.
Without leaves
their slithering branches taper wildly with electric,
cruelly attempting to throttle one another.

Seen more closely this branch
is an unearthly slug, no, a
skin- and moss-clad Green Man
looking hard at you
to steal your worship. But his back
is diseased and infested with parasites.
This one is the shedded skin of snake
still eyeing its prey
on a scattering of gold.

Down on the ground pimples and warts abound
and stones lie apart
visually striking
like the fallen tools of murderers.

And there, black and white in the centre,
what strange and waving creatures
are those?

Ugandan Bestiary

Zebra
Swishing its tail
to keep the flies off its rump
the eyes saying
please don't fill me up again
with terror

Ugandan Cob
The golden year-ringed horn I've lost
proves that
though we're slight
we too can fight –
amongst ourselves

Rothschild Giraffe
Orange and brown
untested like young aristos
we rub our [slightly-shorter] necks
on acacia bark and
against each other's

Cobra
— *Sometimes you will see one*
crossing the track
and see one we did
a black line drawn by God
and a hunger for rats

Silverback
How far can I stretch
my opposable toes today?
You can't see the silver because I recline?
Getting up, the tree I snap's
your back

Hippo
We watch
from the top of the river
eyes deep, in ridges of pink —
just beware
there is a mountain under here

Nile Crocodile

Time
and lazy river heat
lift our traps as we dream
in the certainty of a shape
that lasts forever

Elephant

Skin blackened and slackened by age
tusks long gone
he is outcast on a lonely spit
surrounded by white grebe –
and deathly marabou stork

Great Crested Crane

Red, yellow, black
I am the Ugandan colour bird
and I call out for life
in the golden straw
of her savannah

Exhibition, Merton

– i.m. Jocelyn Merivale

Every Bird is Singing

I watch the painting
with its thousand yellow birds
all edged in black

and only some time later notice
that all their beaks are open,

that every bird
is singing –

*

Green Ghost Girl at No. 9

Who is this green-limned girl
stood at No. 9's red door?

Won't they let her in? Are there
bundles of garlic
splashes of holy water

sprigs of wolfsbane round the frame?

Does some sudden memory
paralyse the will of the dead?

Or perhaps she rehearses her performance,
how with just the right moment and angle
she might make forever good her intent,

push her teetering target
over the edge
of a measureless chasm of fear.

Or maybe she just doesn't have the power
to walk through.

After all there is only so much
the dead can do.

*

The Sea

is everywhere. We are made to think
of our edges, our rocks and shingle beaches

bee-sting Victorian lighthouses —
of hulls on tossed waters
whose fate is to break.

But the sea is also among us
dull green with algae host
sitting, seeping round buildings —

an urge to circumscription
we can entertain, or not.

*

*Found behind the portrait of the baby,
a mental hospital, rain, billowing trees
in iron-dark grey —*

*

— This is my favourite
he tells me, *it reminds me
of the girl I fell in love with.*

A beautiful, everything girl
full of treetop song –

with splashes of red
falling down gold beside her.

Christ in the Crowd

Look at him there with you, now, Christ
walking in the crowd, unaware
of knocking shoulders, heavy-footed
disbelieved and unconcerned. Every bit
as self-absorbed as the next man.
Maybe wondering about a tax return
clinching the latest sale
or a lover who messed him about
last night. Or maybe on the inside
sublime and raging glory.

Christ walking there with you in the crowd.
Keeping quiet as can be,
well away from dodgy metaphors.
Just walking, and worried, like you.

Looking At It Now

– Saint George and the Dragon, Paolo Uccello, 1460,
National Gallery

Knight, you've hit your target
wounded the beast, unruly child, diseased id
with your long, straight, storm-driven pole.
Brow forward, on prancing stead,
your deed is done –
the translucent lipless Princess saved.

But look how she's joined in,
used her girdle to leash the beast
and thwart its fun –
in those Rottweiler eyes
you can see
the final froth of madness
as the horizon recedes –

claws dig into neat turf
wings splay diminished targets

as the poor-dog beast succumbs
between the armoured Nazi Knight
and his Ice Maiden, Nazi wife.

Beast

Look at the beast,
peg-toothed lizard head
pinned down on the ground
by your spear in its neck –

blank coin eye attempting
to look up and around,
ready as ever,
its second nature to fight.

But you've won
George
you've nailed
the lizard

and maybe in your day
with your flat visor
and implacable brow
things were different

but now
it's the beast we feel for –
its dumb, unfettered soul.

iv. Water

Snowflakes Under The Microscope

When it was minus thirty he traipsed Alaska
the Upper Michigan Peninsula
dark Sierra Nevada
searching for the perfect flake.
Bemused Yooper loggers asked
if he ever saw two the same.

He developed a photo-microscope
to show the world
the split and sectored plate,
the rimed crystal,
fernlike stellar dendrite –
all captured in oily-blue,
refracted light.

The six-petal primrose in the midst
of a twelve-branched star
cut his heart.
There was not one light-washed flake
that wasn't perfect –
a micro-blueprint
for a place of worship.

Ice

At night, as you sleep, amorphous slugs of water
stretch silently across the brittle blades of leaves,
to become the chrysalis pins
of ice. Dawn delivers them a colour: white.

The cold air works a somatic spell across the
                                farmer's fields
like a brush over suede, yielding
a new glare, smoking and mist-bright

and making the land seem more like sea,
with ivory bands of grey-flecked foam
drifting across a callous, dark and salted green.

And in the morning as the thaw comes crackling
you walk out and begin to reshape, cone of black,
heart squeezing hot blood and head growling,
strange and beautiful as ice.

Ice, Mist, Qualities of

A misty season.
Words in the mist.
Ice first, then colour.
Shape taken by things.
The quality of hoar, hoariness.
A sliver of river, silver in the mist.
A bulky carr, the image of things.
The quality of where.
Ice leading to shape,
shape emerging from ice.
A hedgelayer
taking his shape from ice.
The quality of a hedgelayer
taking his shape from ice.
The knocking of wood,
tap-knocking of wood.
A straight pole bending.
The hedgelayer breathing
as he cuts at the wood.
A hazel bending,
a hawthorn twisting.

The river in the mist
really a lake.
A white lake in the mist.
The quality of
a white lake in the mist.

Jack

Jack in the dark, fishing the Wandle with Dad.
Some numbers of Jack:
1 (haircut), 11 (age), 7 (fags per day);
3 (Mums, if Edie has her way).

Jack's dad rolls a smoke,
pulls up his tracksuit neck,
but there's no keeping out that damp.
Fetch us that box of bait, Jack…

In the moonlight Jack watches
dimples on the river's surface –
how far they go, spinning,
till something below changes.

Jack might be young,
with a life nobody's after,
but he knows something most
take a lifetime to discover –

impatience is pointless.

Jack waits in the dark,
time unregistered, and ready,
for what might,
or might not, happen next.

Travel

– for S.G.

Yours the first brain I've seen,
white, crinkle-cut,
flashing like a butterfly
across the black screen.

With just enough space to shift
you extract it from our view.

Chased by the transducer
you rotate fast, heroically, revealing
anemone fingers, a quick white heart
two sausage legs,
bowed apart –

you twist, fidget,
try to get away

as if to say
enough of love, light, attention, later –

for now, let me travel
alone in this beautiful dark.

Rise

The vegetation, air is damp.
Branches move slightly
and the sky is grey.
Christmas is coming,
       feel the mind rise.

A blackbird silhouette
jumping under the laurel.
The cut log stained black
with age and rain.
The robin around,
quick with his feathers.
Christmas is…
       …the mind rise.

The river swells, gloomy grey,
and a fox, ears high,
lopes to a sibling,
fidgeting in a daytime dream.
Christmas…
       …rise.

Trip

I drop forward, feel hot skin
replaced by cold, thrashing water.

I realise now it was this
made me get up, escape
the dry, unfocused suburbs of London,
fast-track the buff pelt
of the earth's generous flank

come through the whitewashed seaside town
where I abandoned my clothes
loped down the pebble beach

and waded to this plunge –

where now, with the iron-blue
folding before my eyes
I find myself
again at sea level.

Meeting with Da

Last night again
a dream of Da.

It was a dark shore
and my mother
needed my help
in a ritual to reach him,
her father, in his sick bed,
out some way
through sea.

We trod carefully
on wet pebbles like eggs
that crushed down like mush

then found the link
of safer footing
that would take us out to him.

Side by side
we headed out
under a filthy sky,

nearby the white-flecked
chaos of the waves.

Then I spotted glass —
bright beads and chunks
and the broken necks of phials —
so we placed our bare toes
more tentatively

and finally reached Da's cave.

On a bed on a dais
Da was naked,
brown and dying.

My mother set to nursing him.
After a while
he was able to hold himself up
to kiss me.

I kissed Da.
It was a bloodless kiss
like unminded death.

Last Time

he was here things were a lot more hairy –
invisible fingers plucked cones of water from the

sea

and everywhere the sand was bursting
like puffballs, struck by a flurry of sticks.

Machine guns smacked endlessly at the air
as if its sins were irredeemable,
and the air expressed its pain
with the cries of men, like children.

Lashed by hot grit he'd run like a boy
down the green suede of the Sussex downs, leaping
bodies like the cracked boles of hawthorns,
still fresh with a whorl of flowers –

Now, here again after fifty years,
he can hardly believe this was the place –
the wind's so soft and warm,
the sand and sea don't glisten –

everything seems as banal as home.
He turns to remark to an old friend
but finds that he's fallen several yards back
only to be swiftly enclosed

by a circle of kneeling veterans.

White

i. Ambusher

Salt water drags across the yellow eye
looking up from gloom to light –
fanning out the sun's cascade of rays,
a shadow slithers on the surface –

you are dark, directly below.

With a thrash of the tail rise up fast and smooth,
seize and crush with one savage bite.

Grind a little, then let go –
ambusher.

Retreat to a distance, watch and wait
as your succulent dinner bleeds, slowly, to death.

Rise through unfurling clouds of blood.
Eat, and retreat to the deep to digest.

ii. Curiosity

A large shape on the surface, cutting its splutter.
Rise steadily, slowly, to investigate –
curiosity.

Above the shape something half-formed,
outside of the world, an illusion.
Rise, start to bring up one (left) eye.

Then, on the zenith of the nose,
and in the racing ancient mind,
the sudden stun of bliss,
unmediated, never before known –

then drifting, hypnotised, back into the dark.

For the first time
touched by the hand of man.

A Life at Sea

It was the sea made us free, he said.
Even when things were rough
everything was kept tidy
in Poseidon's chipped-foil sack.

Each day we'd set out in muffled fog
searching for fish, crab, nereid,
only half-aware of what we left behind,
the mainland's weary step.

The work – throwing, pulling, tying, climbing –
was well-defined, it felt like nothing to do –
just watch the horizon's silver needle,
the grand, quiet blending of sun and rain.

With all that space and time
we couldn't help but catch
things behind the mind –
the saltwater feelers of older gods.

There were dull days, storm days,
days when the machinery broke –
but mostly we brought home
all that was required.

I remember once
coming back past the harbour wall,
seagulls dropping on surf, slipping on waves,
the skipper had a moment:
This, above all, boy, he said.
Lash yourself to a story that floats.

This

I hope when they arrive they see this first.
The red-and-white lighthouse
tied to the cliff-top,
the Channel slipping away to reveal
a ribbed parchment of sand
weed-streaked rocks
and space for three men,
an arching rod.

They will not see a horizon.
Rather sea, sky, morning in union,
a relaxing of green and grey,
suffused with childhood blue.

It is beautiful and warm.
I hope this is where they come.
I hope this is what they see.

v. Air

Housemartin

Then
in through the blue window

a housemartin
    hunched up around   .

angelic beating wings

circling the rafters

tensing our naked bodies
as we read
    and drink coffee in bed –

we curl our morning papers,
prepare to drive the thing out.

But
    this bird is no amateur,
doesn't panic in a crisis –

no, this bird
    knows rooms,
is a reader of houses

and sees this one's ours

so retreats quickly
    leaving us with only

the gift
    of the beat
of his wings

    in our hearts.

A Bird on the Moorland

In my dream I was a bird on the moorland.
I saw quick and sure
but with only half an eye.

Free from weight and damage
I moved through a million blistered thorns,
and gorged myself on hidden berries.

I watched dark clouds fill the sky
and sliced through growing winds
to gauge the coming storms.

When the rain fell heavily
I squatted down and ruffled feathers
to reduce the misery of wet.

In the gorgeous midge-thick summer
I swooped my signature in the blank blue sky,
and shrank up small when the great hawks soared.

At dawn and dusk I tipped back my head
and sang loud and well as I could to the heavenly
point at the base of my throat, the world.

Spring Snowfall and Birds

A dogleg in the weather.
Snow means still
but the narrow grey path
between sloping field
and birch and holly wood
is vivid with birds –

blackbird in the middle
straight up the line
with quick wing flicks
black, white
off into the woods –

wren jittery, low
through sparse twigs
each sprig
shielding a secret of its own.

Robin up, swelling, feathery
fluff put forward defiantly –

the snow that falls this spring is small
but it's backed by a damaging wind
and stings –

I walk on down a bitter hill
see shiver a single black leaf of bramble,
the countless good of it all.

Coyote

At first it was the ancient wound
the cut that needed packing.

But it changed, became something else entirely –
the effrontery of it all, a need for total rebuttal.
What that bird meant couldn't go on,
not here, with us, now.

The blue shock of feathers, that ridiculous
undercarriage spinning across the top
of all we desert dwellers had to think and feel,
the way we scraped our lives.

Above all, the dumbass way it beeped.

It was just so damn superior, so free,
like its whole point was to slight the wound.

I hated it and longed to champ
on the crunchy stuff that made up its stupid neck.

So I set another cliff-edge ambush and waited,
a familiar ache at the root of my tongue.

I won't go into it, though.
You've seen this one a thousand times before
and I'll not have you chuckling again
as I try to run on air.

Will-o-wisp

It was easier as a nipper.
Given your first slide rule in senior school
you'd soon work out the sine, cosine or log
with one swift push, and a pull.

Measurement was easy. Just
as you could flip a quick $_3$ to the foot of a C
or pass back a $_2$ to an O

so too could you slap the net with the ball,
top right or top left.

And you knew when to keep your trap shut,
understood when all around you
were silently agreed.

But now you're in a world gone fuzz.
Your conscience, soul, mind, whatever
it is against which you judge
is blurred ground,
rushing away beneath your eyes.

You're out on the marsh at night.
Everything you thought was solid you
has turned out to be
just a trick of the light.

Suburban Alembic

My grandma has peach sheets.
With arms weather-beaten as a sailor's
she hoists them high on a line
where they billow and flap
across Eastbourne's sandy bric-a-brac,
the cool, evening pebble-blue sky.

Coming out from the side passage
the golden dog
spots the sheets
bounces into the bungalow garden
snaps like a puppy
at the dark fuzz of lawn.

Joy. She canters, dives and rolls
into the slap
drop
and leap of the sheets.

She twists and sits up
and barks and barks again:
the dog knows –
the dog knows!

Flight

After furiously roasting the jets
the plane sets off down the runway –
juddering like
she's a little too cheap.
Hangars blotted with rain
appear and swiftly retreat.

Then what should be unimaginable
happens next –

you and all those tense strangers
are scooped up off the ground
going up fast, unsure, unbalanced –

the melange of green and grey –
the road-strapped land –
souping out beneath you,
its gravity tendrils stretching,
snapping as they fail
to wrench you back to safety –

You are freed
whether you like it or not,
and there is no going back.
Watching the flecked blue seat in front
you settle yourself on the surf of fear –

and wait for the perfect light
that comes beyond the clouds.

Printed in Poland
by Amazon Fulfillment
Poland Sp. z o.o., Wrocław